C000082050

DON'T PANIC

· · · · · · · · · · · · · · · · ·
YOU'RE ONLY
· · · · · · · · · · · · · · · · ·

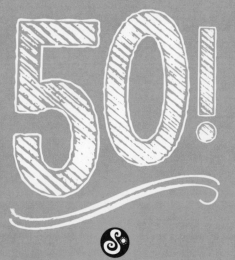

50!

summersdale

DON'T PANIC, YOU'RE ONLY 50!

An Hachette UK Company
www.hachette.co.uk

Summersdale Publishers Ltd
Part of Octopus Publishing Group Limited
Carmelite House
50 Victoria Embankment
LONDON
EC4Y 0DZ

www.summersdale.com

Printed and bound in the Czech Republic

ISBN: 978-1-78685-294-6

Substantial discounts on bulk quantities of Summersdale books are available to corporations, professional associations and other organisations. For details contact general enquiries: telephone: +44 (0) 1243 771107 or email: enquiries@summersdale.com.

TO.......................

FROM....................

CONTENTS

ANOTHER YEAR

OLDER

FOR ALL THE ADVANCES IN MEDICINE, THERE IS STILL NO CURE FOR THE COMMON BIRTHDAY.

JOHN GLENN

HAPPY 20TH
ANNIVERSARY

OF YOUR
30TH
BIRTHDAY!

Anonymous

IT TAKES A LONG TIME TO BECOME YOUNG.

PABLO PICASSO

BY THE TIME WE HIT 50...
WE HAVE LEARNED TO
TAKE LIFE SERIOUSLY,
BUT NEVER OURSELVES.

Marie Dressler

AS A GRADUATE
OF THE ZSA ZSA
GABOR SCHOOL OF
CREATIVE MATHEMATICS,
I HONESTLY DO NOT
KNOW HOW
OLD I AM.

Erma Bombeck

WE'RE VINTAGE!

Jennifer Saunders and Dawn French
on both reaching 50

FORTY IS THE OLD AGE OF YOUTH;

50 THE YOUTH OF OLD AGE.

Victor Hugo

I DON'T FEEL OLD.
I DON'T FEEL ANYTHING
TILL NOON. THAT'S
WHEN IT'S TIME
FOR MY NAP.

BOB HOPE

TO ME, OLD AGE IS
ALWAYS 15 YEARS
OLDER THAN I AM.

Bernard M. Baruch

—

**ABOUT THE ONLY
THING THAT COMES
TO US WITHOUT EFFORT
IS OLD AGE.**

—

GLORIA PITZER

I'D LIKE TO GROW VERY OLD AS SLOWLY AS POSSIBLE.

Charles Lamb

THE WOMAN WHO
TELLS HER AGE IS
EITHER TOO YOUNG
TO HAVE ANYTHING
TO LOSE

OR TOO OLD TO HAVE ANYTHING TO GAIN.

Chinese proverb

HOW OLD WOULD
YOU BE IF YOU
DIDN'T KNOW
HOW OLD
YOU WERE?

Satchel Paige

I REFUSE
TO ADMIT I'M
MORE THAN 52,
EVEN IF THAT DOES
**MAKE MY SONS
ILLEGITIMATE.**

Nancy Astor

FEW WOMEN

ADMIT THEIR AGE.

FEW MEN

ACT THEIRS.

ANONYMOUS

NO WOMAN SHOULD EVER BE QUITE ACCURATE ABOUT HER AGE. IT LOOKS SO CALCULATING.

Oscar Wilde

AGE IS JUST
A NUMBER.
IT'S TOTALLY
IRRELEVANT
UNLESS,
OF COURSE,

YOU HAPPEN TO BE A BOTTLE OF WINE.

Joan Collins

BIRTHDAYS ONLY
COME ONCE A YEAR
UNLESS YOU'RE JOAN
COLLINS, IN WHICH
CASE THEY ONLY
COME EVERY
FOUR YEARS.

STEVE BAUER

JUST WHAT I

ALWAYS WANTED

A FRIEND
NEVER DEFENDS
A HUSBAND WHO GETS
HIS WIFE AN ELECTRIC
SKILLET FOR HER
BIRTHDAY.

Erma Bombeck

—

YESTERDAY IS HISTORY,
TOMORROW IS A
MYSTERY, BUT TODAY
IS A GIFT. THAT IS
WHY IT IS CALLED
THE PRESENT.

—

ELEANOR ROOSEVELT

A HUG IS THE
PERFECT GIFT;
ONE SIZE FITS ALL,
**AND NOBODY
MINDS IF YOU
EXCHANGE IT.**

Anonymous

A GIFT, WITH A KIND
COUNTENANCE, IS A
DOUBLE PRESENT.

Thomas Fuller

A TRUE FRIEND REMEMBERS YOUR BIRTHDAY

**BUT NOT
YOUR AGE.**

Anonymous

YOUTH IS THE GIFT OF NATURE, BUT AGE IS A WORK OF ART.

Garson Kanin

BIRTHDAYS ARE GOOD FOR YOU. STATISTICS SHOW THAT THE PEOPLE WHO HAVE THE MOST LIVE THE LONGEST.

Larry Lorenzoni

THERE ARE 364 DAYS
WHEN YOU MIGHT GET
UN-BIRTHDAY PRESENTS...
AND ONLY ONE FOR
BIRTHDAY PRESENTS,
YOU KNOW.

LEWIS CARROLL

GRIN AND

BEAR IT

WHENEVER THE TALK TURNS TO AGE,

I SAY I
AM 49
PLUS VAT.

Lionel Blair

THE YEARS TEACH MUCH WHICH THE DAYS NEVER KNEW.

Ralph Waldo Emerson

—

AGE IS SOMETHING THAT DOESN'T MATTER, UNLESS YOU ARE A CHEESE.

—

BILLIE BURKE

ANOTHER
BELIEF OF MINE:
THAT EVERYONE ELSE
MY AGE IS AN ADULT,
**WHEREAS I AM MERELY
IN DISGUISE.**

Margaret Atwood

AGEING IS NOT 'LOST YOUTH' BUT A NEW STAGE OF OPPORTUNITY AND STRENGTH.

BETTY FRIEDAN

ONE OF THE BEST PARTS OF GROWING OLDER?

YOU CAN FLIRT ALL YOU LIKE SINCE YOU'VE BECOME HARMLESS.

Liz Smith

**GROWING OLD
IS MANDATORY;
GROWING UP IS
OPTIONAL.**

Chili Davis

ONE OF THE MANY
THINGS NOBODY EVER
TELLS YOU ABOUT MIDDLE
AGE IS THAT IT'S SUCH
A NICE CHANGE FROM
BEING YOUNG.

Dorothy Canfield Fisher

THE LONGER
I LIVE

THE MORE BEAUTIFUL LIFE BECOMES.

Frank Lloyd Wright

OLD AGE IS NO PLACE FOR SISSIES.

Bette Davis

I BELIEVE IN LOYALTY.
WHEN A WOMAN
REACHES A CERTAIN
AGE SHE LIKES, SHE
SHOULD STICK WITH IT.

EVA GABOR

—

ZEAL, N. A CERTAIN
NERVOUS DISORDER
AFFLICTING THE YOUNG
AND INEXPERIENCED.

—

AMBROSE BIERCE

DO A LITTLE

DANCE,

MAKE A

LITTLE LOVE

MIDDLE AGE IS HAVING A CHOICE BETWEEN TWO TEMPTATIONS

AND CHOOSING THE ONE THAT'LL GET YOU HOME EARLIER.

Dan Bennett

I'LL KEEP
SWIVELLING
MY HIPS
UNTIL
THEY NEED
REPLACING.

Tom Jones

OLD PEOPLE
AREN'T EXEMPT
FROM HAVING FUN
AND DANCING.

Liz Smith

IT'S SEX, NOT YOUTH, THAT'S WASTED ON THE YOUNG.

Janet Harris

THE AGEING PROCESS HAS YOU FIRMLY IN ITS GRASP IF YOU NEVER GET THE URGE TO THROW A SNOWBALL.

Doug Larson

YOU KNOW YOU'RE
KNOCKING ON
WHEN YOU FEEL
LIKE THE MORNING-
AFTER-THE-NIGHT-
BEFORE...

**WITHOUT
HAVING BEEN
ANYWHERE.**

Anonymous

THE YOUNG

SOW WILD OATS.

THE OLD GROW

SAGE.

WINSTON CHURCHILL

I'M LIMITLESS AS FAR
AS AGE IS CONCERNED...
AS LONG AS HE HAS A
DRIVER'S LICENCE.

KIM CATTRALL
ON DATING YOUNGER MEN

—

AGE APPEARS TO BE
BEST IN FOUR THINGS -
OLD WOOD BEST TO
BURN, OLD WINE TO
DRINK, OLD FRIENDS
TO TRUST, AND OLD
AUTHORS TO READ.

—

FRANCIS BACON

I DON'T BELIEVE
IN AGEING. I BELIEVE
IN FOREVER ALTERING
ONE'S ASPECT TO
THE SUN. HENCE
MY OPTIMISM.

Virginia Woolf

A MAN IS A FOOL
IF HE DRINKS
BEFORE HE
REACHES 50,

AND A FOOL IF HE DOESN'T DRINK AFTERWARD.

Frank Lloyd Wright

IF YOU THINK
HITTING 40 IS
LIBERATING,
**WAIT TILL YOU
HIT 50.**

Michelle Pfeiffer

YOUNG AT HEART

I'M AIMING
BY THE TIME I'M
50 TO STOP BEING
AN ADOLESCENT.

Wendy Cope

YOU CAN'T
TURN BACK THE
CLOCK, BUT YOU
CAN WIND IT
UP AGAIN.

Bonnie Prudden

THE OLD
BELIEVE
EVERYTHING;
THE MIDDLE-
AGED SUSPECT
EVERYTHING;

THE YOUNG KNOW EVERYTHING.

Oscar Wilde

CHILDREN ARE A GREAT COMFORT IN YOUR OLD AGE – AND THEY HELP YOU REACH IT FASTER, TOO.

Lionel Kauffman

MY MOTHER IS
GOING TO HAVE TO
STOP LYING ABOUT HER
AGE BECAUSE PRETTY
SOON I'M GOING TO BE
OLDER THAN SHE IS.

TRIPP EVANS

—

AS IS A TALE, SO IS LIFE:
NOT HOW LONG IT IS,
BUT HOW GOOD IT IS,
IS WHAT MATTERS.

—

SENECA

A MAN
IS NOT OLD
AS LONG AS
HE IS SEEKING
SOMETHING.

Jean Rostand

TO GET BACK MY
YOUTH I WOULD
DO ANYTHING
IN THE WORLD,

EXCEPT TAKE EXERCISE, GET UP EARLY, OR BE RESPECTABLE.

Oscar Wilde

THE GREAT THING

ABOUT GETTING OLDER IS THAT

YOU DON'T LOSE

ALL THE OTHER AGES YOU'VE BEEN.

MADELEINE L'ENGLE

TO KEEP THE
HEART UNWRINKLED,
TO BE HOPEFUL,
KINDLY, CHEERFUL,
REVERENT – THAT IS
**TO TRIUMPH OVER
OLD AGE.**

Thomas Bailey Aldrich

OLDER AND

WISER?

NONE ARE SO OLD AS THOSE WHO HAVE OUTLIVED ENTHUSIASM.

Henry David Thoreau

THE BEST WAY TO GET MOST HUSBANDS TO DO SOMETHING

IS TO SUGGEST THAT PERHAPS THEY'RE TOO OLD TO DO IT.

Anne Bancroft

THE SURPRISING
THING ABOUT YOUNG
FOOLS IS HOW MANY
SURVIVE TO BECOME
OLD FOOLS.

Doug Larson

I HAVE ENJOYED
GREATLY THE SECOND
BLOOMING... SUDDENLY
YOU FIND – AT THE AGE
OF 50, SAY – THAT A
WHOLE NEW LIFE HAS
OPENED BEFORE YOU.

AGATHA CHRISTIE

—

OLD MEN ARE FOND
OF GIVING GOOD
ADVICE, TO CONSOLE
THEMSELVES FOR
BEING NO LONGER IN
A POSITION TO GIVE
BAD EXAMPLES.

—

FRANÇOIS DE LA ROCHEFOUCAULD

TO KNOW HOW
TO GROW OLD IS
THE MASTER-WORK
OF WISDOM.

Henri-Frédéric Amiel

YOU ARE ONLY
YOUNG ONCE,

BUT YOU CAN BE IMMATURE FOR A LIFETIME.

John P. Grier

HE'S SO OLD THAT
WHEN HE ORDERS
A 3-MINUTE EGG, THEY
**ASK FOR THE
MONEY UP FRONT.**

Milton Berle

OLD AGE PUTS MORE WRINKLES IN OUR MINDS THAN ON OUR FACES.

Michel de Montaigne

ONE OF THE SIGNS
OF PASSING YOUTH IS
THE BIRTH OF A SENSE
OF FELLOWSHIP WITH
OTHER HUMAN BEINGS
AS WE TAKE OUR PLACE
AMONG THEM.

Virginia Woolf

NO MAN IS EVER OLD ENOUGH TO KNOW BETTER.

Holbrook Jackson

WHEN I WAS A BOY OF 14, MY FATHER WAS SO IGNORANT I COULD HARDLY STAND TO HAVE THE OLD MAN AROUND.

BUT WHEN
I GOT TO
21, I WAS
ASTONISHED
AT HOW
MUCH HE HAD
LEARNED IN
SEVEN YEARS.

Mark Twain

LIVE, LOVE

AND

LAST

HE WHO
LAUGHS, LASTS!

MARY PETTIBONE POOLE

—

TOMORROW'S GONE - WE'LL HAVE TONIGHT!

DOROTHY PARKER

—

TO STOP
AGEING
–
KEEP ON
RAGING.

MICHAEL FORBES

THE OTHER DAY
A MAN ASKED ME
WHAT I THOUGHT
WAS THE BEST
TIME OF LIFE.

'WHY,' I ANSWERED...
'NOW.'

David Grayson

NO MATTER HOW
OLD YOU ARE, THERE'S
ALWAYS SOMETHING
GOOD TO LOOK
FORWARD TO.

Lynn Johnston

THE FOLLIES
WHICH A MAN
REGRETS MOST IN HIS
LIFE ARE THOSE WHICH
HE DIDN'T COMMIT
**WHEN HE HAD THE
OPPORTUNITY.**

Helen Rowland

ONE CAN
REMAIN ALIVE
LONG PAST THE USUAL
DATE OF DISINTEGRATION
IF ONE IS UNAFRAID OF
CHANGE, INSATIABLE
IN INTELLECTUAL
CURIOSITY, INTERESTED
IN BIG THINGS,
AND HAPPY IN
SMALL WAYS.

Edith Wharton

JUST REMEMBER,
ONCE YOU'RE OVER
THE HILL YOU BEGIN
TO PICK UP SPEED.

Charles M. Schulz

MIDDLE AGE IS WHEN WE CAN DO JUST AS MUCH AS EVER

– BUT WOULD RATHER NOT.

Anonymous

THE TIME TO BEGIN MOST THINGS IS 10 YEARS AGO.

Mignon McLaughlin

NOBODY GROWS
OLD MERELY BY
LIVING A NUMBER OF
YEARS. WE GROW
OLD BY DESERTING
OUR IDEALS.

SAMUEL ULLMAN

THE
PURPOSE
OF LIFE IS
TO FIGHT
MATURITY.

Dick Werthimer

—

AGE DOES
NOT PROTECT YOU
FROM LOVE. BUT LOVE,
TO SOME EXTENT,
PROTECTS YOU
FROM AGE.

—

Jeanne Moreau

WE KNOW WE'RE
GETTING OLD
WHEN THE ONLY
THING WE WANT
FOR OUR BIRTHDAY

IS NOT TO BE
REMINDED OF IT.

Anonymous

MAY YOU
LIVE
ALL THE DAYS OF
YOUR LIFE.

JONATHAN SWIFT

THE AVERAGE CHILD
LAUGHS ABOUT 400 TIMES
PER DAY; THE AVERAGE
ADULT LAUGHS ONLY 15
TIMES PER DAY. WHAT
HAPPENED TO THE
OTHER 385 LAUGHS?
LAUGH AND LIVE!

Anonymous

TIME DOTH FLIT; OH SH*T!

Dorothy Parker

ILLS, PILLS

AND

TWINGES

MY DOCTOR
TOLD ME TO DO
SOMETHING
THAT PUTS
ME OUT OF
BREATH,

SO I'VE TAKEN UP SMOKING AGAIN.

Jo Brand

YOU KNOW
YOU'VE REACHED
MIDDLE-AGE WHEN
YOUR WEIGHTLIFTING
CONSISTS MERELY
OF STANDING UP.

BOB HOPE

**MIDDLE AGE IS
WHEN YOU CHOOSE
YOUR CEREAL FOR
THE FIBRE, NOT
THE TOY.**

Anonymous

—

THE YEARS
BETWEEN 50 AND
70 ARE THE HARDEST.
YOU ARE ALWAYS BEING
ASKED TO DO MORE,
AND YOU ARE NOT YET
DECREPIT ENOUGH TO
TURN THEM DOWN.

—

T. S. ELIOT

I WOULD RATHER
BE ROUND AND
JOLLY THAN THIN
AND CROSS.

Ann Widdecombe

IF I'D KNOWN
I WAS GOING
TO LIVE THIS
LONG,

I'D HAVE TAKEN
BETTER CARE
OF MYSELF.

Eubie Blake

I FEEL STRONGER
NOW THAN
MAYBE 20
YEARS AGO.
IF YOUR MIND
IS STRONG,
YOUR BODY WILL
BE STRONG.

Madonna

I DON'T WANT A FLU JAB.
I LIKE GETTING FLU.
IT GIVES ME SOMETHING
**ELSE TO COMPLAIN
ABOUT**.

David Letterman

MIDDLE AGE IS
THE TIME WHEN A MAN
IS ALWAYS THINKING IN
A WEEK OR TWO HE WILL
FEEL AS GOOD AS EVER.

Don Marquis

I NEVER
WORRY ABOUT
DIETS. THE ONLY
CARROTS THAT
INTEREST ME ARE
THE NUMBER YOU
GET IN A DIAMOND.

Mae West

PEOPLE WHO SAY YOU'RE JUST AS **OLD AS YOU FEEL** ARE ALL WRONG, **FORTUNATELY.**

RUSSELL BAKER

AS YOU GET OLDER
THREE THINGS HAPPEN.
THE FIRST IS YOUR
MEMORY GOES, AND I
CAN'T REMEMBER THE
OTHER TWO...

NORMAN WISDOM

AGE SELDOM ARRIVES SMOOTHLY OR QUICKLY.

IT'S MORE
OFTEN A
SUCCESSION
OF JERKS.

Jean Rhys

WHAT MOST
PERSONS CONSIDER
AS VIRTUE, AFTER
THE AGE OF 40 IS
SIMPLY A LOSS
OF ENERGY.

Voltaire

—

OLD MINDS ARE LIKE
OLD HORSES; YOU MUST
EXERCISE THEM IF YOU
WISH TO KEEP THEM IN
WORKING ORDER.

—

JOHN QUINCY ADAMS

YOU KNOW YOU'RE
GETTING OLD WHEN
YOU STOP TO TIE
YOUR SHOES

AND WONDER
WHAT ELSE YOU CAN
DO WHILE YOU'RE
DOWN THERE.

George Burns

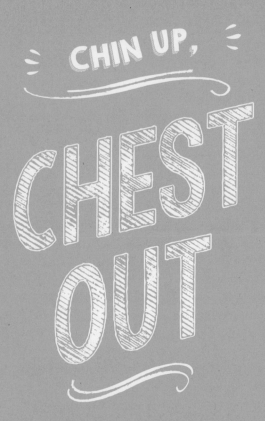

CHIN UP, CHEST OUT

YOU CAN ONLY
PERCEIVE REAL BEAUTY
IN A PERSON AS THEY
GET OLDER.

Anouk Aimée

MIDDLE AGE IS
WHEN YOUR AGE
STARTS TO SHOW
AROUND YOUR
MIDDLE.

Bob Hope

**THE AGE OF
A WOMAN DOESN'T
MEAN A THING. THE BEST
TUNES ARE PLAYED ON
THE OLDEST FIDDLES.**

Ralph Waldo Emerson

I DON'T PLAN TO GROW OLD GRACEFULLY;

I PLAN
TO HAVE
FACELIFTS
UNTIL MY
EARS MEET.

Rita Rudner

REGRETS ARE THE NATURAL PROPERTY OF GREY HAIRS.

Charles Dickens

**PLEASE DON'T
RETOUCH MY WRINKLES.
IT TOOK ME SO LONG
TO EARN THEM.**

ANNA MAGNANI

WHEN IT
COMES TO
STAYING YOUNG,
A MIND-LIFT
BEATS A FACE-
LIFT ANY DAY.

Marty Bucella

—

THERE IS ONLY ONE
CURE FOR GREY HAIR.
IT WAS INVENTED
BY A FRENCHMAN.
IT IS CALLED THE
GUILLOTINE.

—

P. G. WODEHOUSE

I'M LIKE OLD WINE.
THEY DON'T BRING
ME OUT VERY
OFTEN,

BUT I'M WELL

PRESERVED.

Rose Kennedy

I'M NOT
DENYING MY AGE,
I'M EMBELLISHING
MY YOUTH.

Tamara Reynolds

MIDDLE AGE IS YOUTH
WITHOUT LEVITY,
AND AGE WITHOUT
DECAY.

DANIEL DEFOE

NATURE GIVES YOU
THE FACE YOU HAVE
AT 20, BUT IT'S UP TO
YOU TO MERIT THE FACE
YOU HAVE AT 50.

Coco Chanel

SHE WAS A
HANDSOME WOMAN
OF 45 AND WOULD
REMAIN SO FOR
MANY YEARS.

Anita Brookner

THE SECRET OF STAYING YOUNG IS TO LIVE HONESTLY, EAT SLOWLY

AND LIE ABOUT YOUR AGE.

Lucille Ball

If you're interested in finding out more about our books, find us on Facebook at **Summersdale Publishers** and follow us on Twitter at **@Summersdale**.

www.summersdale.com